Silencing Our Imposter

Hearing Our Heart Beyond the Noise

To Dale,
Thanks for your friendship and wise exhortations over the years!

Jim May

Jim May

Silencing Our Imposter
Hearing Our Heart Beyond the Noise

v2.0

Cover design by Tristan Mraz
Cover image by istockphoto.com

Outskirts Press, Inc.
http://www.outskirtspress.com

ISBN: 978-1-4787-2125-3

PRINTED IN THE UNITED STATES OF AMERICA

*"Human beings live in a cell of their own creation,
And almost everybody is content to rearrange the
furniture in their prison cell and call it freedom."*

(George Gurdeiff)

Table of Contents

Acknowledgments

To my wife Maureen who has stuck with me for forty-seven years, and recently was my wonderful nurse helping me to recover from open heart surgery. Thanks to my "magnificent princess."

Special thanks To Darrell and Sandy Scott and the Rachel's Challenge Family. Darrell's previous research, hours of brainstorming, and counsel have challenged me to go deeper. Many of the ideas in this book started with our study together. Thanks for your friendship and love.

The gifted and humble staff and presenters at Rachel's Challenge have come together to impact the world with kindness and compassion. But even beyond that lofty achievement, their openness and depth of thinking have given me many thoughts to ponder and pursue. Thank you for taking me into your lives.

Thanks to Tristan Mraz for his cover design.

FINDING JIM

I was there from the start
This child they called "Jim."
Fit for only one part
In a play from my heart

I was who I was
Past moments forgotten
Present seconds enjoyed
The future unemployed

Freedom was real
Riding my wheels
Leaning into the curves
Along Brush Creek

To grab an afternoon snack
Of peanut butter and jelly
On my way to Bobby's
To mess around with my buddy

But as I grew up
The bike was parked
And the route was restricted
By other's directions

I could not escape the places
Where I wore other's faces
To look as I should
Not be as I be

Where I was taught
To speak with borrowed voices
Learning lines to a play
That did not fit my way

I was told the other fashions
Would help me be respected
To be accepted
And not be rejected

I wanted to be liked -
Loved and adored
So I dressed for effect
To be part of the elect

I tried the foreign tongue
But absorbing strange words
Was unnatural to my style
Imported to my smile

And "Jim" was buried
Under other's inventions
Living by the rules
And all the conventions

I wondered who was this "Jim?"
A doctor for my family?
A salesman for my fortune?
A believer for my faith?

My outside pulled from my inside
Which mask did I fit?

I was bent back and forth
And finally I did break

I was in pieces
Lying on the ground
A puzzle not together
Living other's ideas

How could I come together?
Inside matching out?
Not lying here in fragments
Wondering how to get about.

I decided the way was back
To the place I had been
To find the freedom I lack
And ride that bike again.

Because the "Jim" I was
Is who I am meant to be
Not conformed to the prison
Of other's thoughts of me

On the journey back to "Jim"
I left the world of illusions
And walked into a new dimension
A kingdom with no delusions

It supported me on my walk
With no deceptive talk
It applauded my progression
And blocked steps of regression

It maintained my amateur standing
Letting me work for love, not wealth
I was connected with others
Not as competitors, but as mates

Each in their unique place
Walking their personal pace
With significance and grace
Connecting face to face

I found the best room where I fit
For to help a redundant race
Is to be an original, not a copy
And occupy my special place.

Introduction

There is a unique, gifted, and significant True Person in all of us that wants to be free.

This True Person is:

Already in harmony with all other True Persons around us.

Already one with nature.

Already finely tuned to discern truth from error.

Already a trustworthy counselor and guide for our lives.

Already has a special place and purpose in life.

Already connected with all truth of history past and present.

The problem is this Person has been hidden by the deceptions of an Imposter self that has hijacked our identity.

Powerful emotions from family and culture have promoted lies about who we are and shouted down the voice of our True Person.

The world has pushed us into groups to define and control us diluting our uniqueness.

The education system has put us on "tracks" leading away from our distinctive callings.

The religious systems have dictated what we should believe for acceptance, creating "we" and "them" camps everywhere we turn.

The political system gives us only two choices that force compromise with our consciences.

The labels put on the outside make us uncomfortable inside.

The uniforms we wear never quite fit.

"Give me liberty or give me death," is not just the cry of Patrick Henry. It is the cry of every Person hidden behind Imposter's lies and the world's collectives.

Have you noticed a stirring in your heart to break out of the labels and groups that don't define you?

Are you tired of playing a role in life that doesn't fit?

Do you sense there is a real person inside you that has been covered by the dirt of fabrications you have believed all your life?

Do you desperately want to find out your true identity that has been hijacked by an Imposter self?

If so, then, you are already part of the growing revolution around you.

You are not alone.

This revolution is the Person breaking through the barricades of stale and oppressive systems that have enslaved us.

It is not a revolution of rock-throwing, placard-waving and screaming speeches.

Those revolutions are just systems of revolt that further enslave the person.

This revolution is peaceful, unstoppable and the next great step in the journey of mankind.

It is irresistible because man can't live in his own prison systems, and will burst out into liberty.

Man's systems are crumbling around us, and the Person is emerging.

To be sure, this revolution has been going on throughout human history, but has intensified recently with the explosion of technology, giving more power to those who would control us.

Remember the "high tech, high touch" of John Naisbitt's,

"Megatrends" (1982)? His contention was that the more technology closes in on the human spirit, the more we need human touch. Since Naisbitt's book came out, technology has advanced exponentially, and given collective systems even greater power to control us. But the human spirit cannot live in the houses collectivism has built for us. We will fight to the death for our liberty from technological oppression.

"High touch" is increasing.

People are taking the risk of transparency.

Small groups of honest seekers are forming.

Persons are abandoning institutionalized religion.

Brave souls are striking out from educational "tracking."

The human spirit demands freedom.

As I neared the completion of this book, I was taken in for open heart surgery to receive 6 bypasses. As I was coming out of recovery, I noticed something had changed in my heart – not just physically, but spiritually. I was closer to everyone. I felt hearts around me. It's like the bypasses went around old, clogged arteries and tapped into a new Source. I was connected. The surprise to me was that I was not trying to make it happen. It happened when I was not looking. Nature lined up behind me and connected me to others in a deeper way.

My spirit was fighting for "high touch" even when I was totally sedated for surgery! Our True Self united with nature is a powerful force and cannot be stopped from emerging from collective systems, our Imposters lies, and technological control.

This book is about how to silence our Imposter and hear our hearts. It is written from personal experience to keep it as close to practical as possible. My hope is to help others be set free to "be who they be," because any other way is death to our souls.

Jim May

Why Are We Killing Ourselves?

"Have no fear of robbers or murderers. Such dangers are without, and are but petty. We should fear ourselves. Prejudices are the real robbers, vices the real murderers. The great dangers are within us. What matters it what threatens our heads or our purses? Let us think only of what threatens our souls."

(Victor Hugo, "Les Miserables")

Why don't some people want to live anymore – even the successful and wealthy?

The tragic suicide of all-pro linebacker Junior Seau raised many questions. He was admired and respected for his out-going personality, generous nature and success in football. Yet he chose not to live any longer in this world. Why? Speculations range from concussion induced brain damage, to hidden depression caused by retiring from the exciting world of pro football, but no one knows.

There are over 34,600 deaths by suicide every year in America, and over 375,000 attempts.

This is staggering. Suicide is the third leading cause of death among teens behind auto accidents and homicides.

What is going on here?

Why do so many not want to live anymore?

Why did I get to that point myself?

Why are we killing ourselves?

I don't necessarily mean we are putting a gun to our head (although some are in record numbers), but we can kill ourselves with subtle put downs:

I'm stupid,

I'm useless,

I don't deserve it,

I never do anything right,

I'm not as good as them,

I'm worthless.

You know the list of subtle forms of suicide we speak in our heads.

Then we try to drown out the depressing voices.

Making food our comfort,

Using drugs and alcohol to forget,

Smoking to relax,

Getting pets that like us,

Blaming others for the hand we have been dealt,

Losing ourselves in endless, empty TV shows,

Pretending to be our idols in sports and movies,

Or we can be someone else on Facebook.

My own fantasy of escape is imagining I can play the guitar or the piano with such skill that people are sitting around me in awe of my talent.

Anyway, I digress.

Back to the point…

Self-hate can escalate and get violent by cutting, shooting or jumping to our death, and we all know that anger with ourselves can turn violent against others.

Why are we killing ourselves when wisdom is crying out to save us from death?

When I graduated from college a wise teacher wrote to me that wisdom was calling out to us everywhere we look. Our job is to take time to listen. It is there, if we pay attention.

It's like two men who were walking together through busy, noisy, downtown New York City. One of them, a Native American, suddenly stopped and said, "Did you hear that?"

"Hear what?"

"The cricket!"

"What cricket?" With all the noise of the traffic, people on cell phones, and construction, the man could not hear the cricket. The Native American walked to a tiny potted plant in front of a store and bent down.

"Hear it now?"

"Yes! How did you do that?"

"You have to listen beyond the noise."

The Native American had trained his ear to listen beyond all the background noises.

My wise teacher concluded his exhortation saying that those who don't listen to wisdom will injure themselves.

Then he said something almost shocking:

Those who hate wisdom love death.

Those are strong words: "injures themselves" – "loves death."

Really? This is serious business.

So I ask: "Why do we love death over wisdom and life?"

We know the principles of natural law:

We reap what we sow.

We get back what we give out.

We are judged by our own judgments.

We attract what we project and believe.

So why do we not turn these principles to our benefit instead of our hurt?

Here's what I think...

Maybe we are trying to kill the wrong person.

What if the person we are trying to kill is not us?

What if the person we are trying to kill is already dead?

What if the person we don't like is just an illusion molded by cultural, family and personal lies?

What if he is an Imposter shaped by a sick world, distorted opinions, and false judgments?

What if we have come to believe the lies about us and believe they are us?

What if we have been repeating them over and over in our heads?

What if lies have become our truth and we are living in illusions?

What if our Imposter is telling us we want things we don't need that leave us empty when we get them?

The lastest iphone,

Computer,

Downloaded game,

Car with our favorite color,

Or sneakers.

You name it, big or small, expensive or cheap, there is no material thing that can fill an empty heart.

What if our Imposter is telling us we need things that will harm us?

A puff of weed,

A shot of heroine,

A bullet to the head.

In that case, we are seeking to execute the wrong person!

You want to hear some good news?

We all have an alternative – another person.

There is a True Self hidden behind our Imposter.

This person is beautiful, unique, significant, special, needed, and loved.

There is a person inside us that is worthwhile and worth saving.

This person is truly likeable, fun loving, and happy.

So the question is…

What if we don't have to kill ourselves, because we like who we are?

A mind-bending idea hit me in the face, and changed my perspective.

It set me free from my Imposter's prison of lies.

When I first heard it, I did not understand.

It took me six months to "see" it.

Here it is…

We are not our story or our thoughts.

Our story is merely what we have experienced, not who we are.

Our thoughts can be lies or truth, but they are not who we are either.

So who are we?

We are the observer of our thoughts and story.

We can step back and take a look at
What we are thinking and
What has happened to us.

We can stop defining ourselves from our thoughts and stories.

We can identify the lies in our heads telling us we are victims, worthless, and stupid.

We can stop comparing ourselves with others and wanting to be someone else.

We can mute the voices of others trying to tell us who we are.

We can refuse to be blackmailed by others who withdraw friendship if we don't conform.

We can silence the voices of the cultural collectives around us telling us who we are...

For example,

Educationally being put on "tracks" in trains all going to the same destination,

Religiously being forced into narrow-minded dogma to be accepted,

Politically being forced into one of two parties, that don't define what we really believe.

We can observe...

That's not me!

You can tell the teacher you are not just a student,
The government you are not just a citizen,
The polls you are not just an opinion,
You can tell those with false judgments,
distorted opinions,
and your own Imposter,

"THAT IS NOT ME!"

"I AM WHO I AM!"

SO WHO ARE YOU – REALLY?

How can you find out?

This may not be easy.

It requires getting quiet, narrowing down the voices and listening to your heart.

Who we are comes from an honest heart.

Get in the space between your thoughts and let your True Self discern truth and error.

Our True Self is good at filtering what is true and false.

Some call it instinct.

Some call it "gut check."

Some call it "seeing through."

Whatever we call, it is our True Self seeing reality behind the illusions and truth behind the lies.

When we hear the truth from inside, we can counter the lies of our Imposter.

Do not underestimate the power of exposing the lies and seeing the truth.

When you "see," it is done.

You don't have to work to make it happen.

"Seeing" makes it happen.

Lies have power only in the dark. When the light exposes them, they dissolve.

Remember our True Self is the good self.

We all have a struggle sometimes doing what is right or sometimes we do the wrong thing.

However, the fact that we want to do what is right says there is good in us.

So where is the bad stuff coming from?

Who is telling us ways to be happy that instead make us miserable?

It is that Imposter.

The irony is this Imposter is an illusion, absorbing delusions from outside voices.

So we when we try kill him with put-downs, we are trying to kill a dead man. It's like going to a cemetery, digging up a grave and talking to dead bones. Or it is like pulling a casket out of the back of a hearse and opening it to talk to a decayed body!

Pretty silly, but we have all done it many times.

Then why is this illusion running our lives?

He lives through our memories and emotions telling us those lies – "You are worthless, stupid, useless... etc."

Emotional memories can be very powerful.

One time I barely escaped a serious collision at an intersection in Denver. I missed a red light, began to run through it. I glanced to my right and saw a car barreling down a freeway off ramp, and jammed on my breaks stopping a foot from disaster.

So why do I tell you this story? Every time I come to this intersection, it raises powerful emotions about that narrow escape. I remember every detail, think what could have happened and fear seizes me. Even though the event is long past, the emotions of that moment come back.

There are other places like that in my life – some negative, some positive. Pleasant emotions rise up in me when I look at mountains I have climbed in Rocky Mountain National Park; or when I pass our tiny home where we raised our kids.

Others have shared similar experiences.

It is universal.

And the point is that memories can trigger powerful emotions – some of which can be very destructive being built on false illusions, telling us we are stupid or worthless, etc. These emotional illusions can come from any direction friends, family, culture, school, or work. They can be very debilitating and take over our true identity and lock us in a prison of lies, never letting us experience who we are.

So what is the best weapon against lies?

TRUTH!

The great thing about truth is it always wins over lies.

Our true person knows when it hears truth and when it is being fed lies.

Our True Self has a great filter system.

So we find out who we really are by silencing the lies and believing the truth.

Dead Man Yelling

"Man has a body which is at once his burden and his temptation. He drags it along and yields to it."

(Victor Hugo, "Les Miserables")

Who's yelling at us robbing us of sleep with worries about the future?

Who's making us sick with guilt about the past?

Who's obsessing about what others think about us?

Who's letting bullies intimidate us?

Who's keeping me awake debating political rivals who don't even know I exist and don't care.

Who's escalating, irrational arguments between couples?

Who's keeping us from connecting in heart?

Who's robbing us of the joy of the present?

Who's dividing our country with deception, suspicion and hate?

Who's inflaming world leaders to start wars?

He has various aliases:

The Personage,

The Pain Body,

The False Self,

The Ego.

I call him Dead Man Yelling, because he is only a thought – bad memories and lies.

He is the false self we created to deal with our pain and hurts.

He instigates "fight or flight." He eggs some on to fight with such weapons as anger, vengeance, retaliation, competition, and violence in words or action.

He tells others to "fly away" into such things as withdrawal, depression, defeat, self-deprecation, and even suicide.

This Imposter is a shadow, a fake version of our self.

He can fake happiness with a fake smile,

Fake enthusiasm when we are bored,

Fake being nice when feeling anger,

Fake being a "good boy" to please parents and church people, when inside he doesn't believe what he "should," only to find out in the end that we are never good enough.

He can make himself look like us, but is not really us.

In truth, he lives in constant fear, consumed with getting other's approval.

Most of all our Imposter is a liar, a very clever one.

He can twist and turn us in any direction to get control.

This cagy Imposter can take over our identity, bury our True Self and make us act out of what we are not.

The Imposter can hijack our identity and make our dysfunction seem normal.

As a result…

We don't know who we are or where we fit.

We are out of sync with the unity of the universe.

We can't connect with each other.

We seem to have learned the wrong lines for the play we are in and people are booing us off the stage.

We are alone and alienated.

Sociologically we are alienated from others, because we communicate through our Imposters.

Ecologically we are alienated from creation, because we are not lined up with natural laws.

Psychologically we are alienated from ourselves, because our Imposter has stolen our identity.

Spiritually we are alienated from the Source, Guide and Goal of all things.

Children curse and disrespect their parents.

Parents don't recognize the person their child has become.

Confusion, dysfunction, and disconnection invade family circles.

Couples can't communicate on the same plane.

Mothers say of wayward sons and daughters, "That is not the child I know."

Politicians talk in riddles twisting truth.

Religions fracture over trivialities.

Nations go into wars nobody wants.

The world becomes irrational and plunges into the madness of inquisitions and genocides.

"If the history of humanity were the clinical case history of a single human being, the diagnosis would have to be: chronic paranoid delusions, a pathological propensity to commit murder and acts of extreme violence and cruelty against his perceived "enemies"—his own unconsciousness projected outward. Criminally insane, with a few brief lucid intervals." (Eckhart Tolle)

And Parker Palmer adds, *"Afraid that our inner light will be extinguished or our inner darkness will be exposed, we hide our true identities from each other. In the process, we become separated from our own souls. We end up living divided lives, so far from the truth we hold within that we cannot know the integrity that comes from being what we are."*

And all this is accomplished by a fictitious Imposter that exists only in our thoughts fed by the powerful emotions of past experiences.

He convinces us he is who we are.

Is there a way out of the grip of the Imposter?

Yes!

I can personally confirm it, because a steady peace has settled over my wife and I since we discovered one basic truth as:

We are not our story or our thoughts, but the observer of them.

I got to a point where I was questioning the veracity of my thoughts and came to the conclusion that my thoughts were not who I was.

Confronting My Imposter

"Jean Valjean was found guilty; the terms of the code were explicit; in our civilization there are fearful hours; such are those when the criminal law pronounces shipwreck upon a man. What a mournful moment is that in which society withdraws itself and gives up a thinking being forever... He was no longer Jean Valjean; he was Number 24601."

(Victor Hugo, "Les Miserables")

Why was I so angry?
I was exploding in foul language at
my cursor randomly skipping on my computer,
writing addresses wrong,
spilling my coffee,
losing five games of chess on the computer,
Kansas losing in the NCAA basketball tournament,
Silly, small things.

A buddy told me old guys like me explode more often because they no longer have the energy to hold down their anger. That made sense to me, because the older I got, the angrier I got.

I imagined myself speaking at a conference, dropping my notes and exploding in profanity, ruining my reputation forever.

I had to get a handle on this.

Three men in different words encouraged me to think about the root cause of my anger.

They told me to find the lie behind my rage.

That was a revolutionary thought.

There is a lie behind my anger?

But what was the lie?

How could I identify it?

The answer came three days later as I observed my thoughts.

The lie was exposed when I dropped my toast, jam side down, on the floor.

(The "three second rule" of picking it up and eating it does not apply when it lands jam side down. The dirt sticks and you have to clean it up and throw it away!)

So I launched into my usual rant with a lot of profanity.

I was glad it was winter, the windows were closed, and my neighbors didn't hear my diatribe, and my "good guy" image remained intact.

Somewhere in my tirade, I yelled,

"YOU IDIOT!"

And there it was – the lie I had believed most of my life.

I remembered past incidents that confirmed the lie that I was an idiot.

I thought of the time my mom took me to a special school in Kansas City to improve my reading skills. I was in high school and very embarrassed that I was seen as a poor reader.

In my head, I heard, "You're an idiot! You can't read!"

The lie was reinforced over the years, living with what I perceived were genius siblings. My grades never measured up to theirs. Next to their straight "A's," my "B's" and "C's" looked like "F's."

The lie magnified when my mom seemed to give me a look

of intellectual superiority when she was correcting my writing or spelling.

Then the ultimate humiliation came when my parents sent me to a small college in Illinois because "I was not ready for the big University of Kansas."

"Not ready" was translated in my mind, "you're an idiot." So the lie continued.

I could never seem to concentrate on tests in school, because I was thinking I was a dummy and couldn't measure up to students around me. Also, I was thinking about passing the test instead of concentrating on the questions being asked. The bad test scores only confirmed my belief that I was stupid.

School was a prison of depression and defeat.

Over the years, I reinforced the lie by interpreting events to support my assumption. For example, if I could not repair something, I called myself a mechanical moron. It was said with humor, but there was hurt underneath. It was all subconscious, but very real.

Believing the lie that I was an idiot hurt my communication with my wife. She grew up with two brothers and confrontation was second nature to her. She is a very secure and strong person.

So when she questioned or confronted me, I thought she was calling me an idiot.

When she said, "Turn right," I heard, "Turn right, you idiot!"

I usually reacted in anger or retaliated with my silent treatment to bug her.

She did not have the remotest thought she was calling me an idiot, but I took it that way, because I had believed the lie.

Even the past few years, I was reluctant to submit my books to a publisher, because I thought they were not good enough. While I was writing, thoughts would come to my mind like, "No one will read this stuff," or "there is a book in Barnes & Noble that has covered this subject far better" or "just quit, no one is interested."

Maintaining the discipline of writing is hard enough without these negative thoughts.

But then I finally saw the lie.

The amazing thing was seeing the truth of the lie set me free from it.

It did not take long, expensive hours in the office of a psychologist.

Seeing truth and exposing lies is the best therapy, and we all have an "inner counselor" we can rely on.

This "inner counselor" is the observer of our thoughts and stories.

He senses the difference between lies and truth.

The more we let our True Self observe, the better he gets at discerning.

Bringing the lie out of the darkness into the light reduced its power over me. It was encouraging to see how fast a six-decade problem could be conquered. I did not have to recount my entire past to weed the garden of my mind. It was quick and simple.

Lies dissolve when exposed.

Light has tremendous power.

But I had to take another step to complete the process...

I had to replace the lie with the truth.

So, I began to listen to my True Self to uncover my real identity.

I remembered a time I gave a speech in front of my peers in a fraternity at UCLA. A teacher I greatly respected was there. Afterwards he put his arm around my shoulder and said, "Jim, you are a good teacher."

The irony was, I was not trying to teach, but just sharing my experience. I didn't think I was teaching, but my respected mentor saw something in me that I didn't know about myself.

Let's pause here and think about how powerful words are. Here was one word telling me I was an idiot and another telling me I was a good teacher. One was a lie, the other was the truth.

Both strains followed me throughout life, and each became dominant depending on who was in control of my thoughts – my Imposter or my True Self. So I had confidence to teach, but could easily revert back to the lie and say, "that was a stupid thing to say." Then I would worry about what people thought of me.

This dualistic state between lies and truth affects us all, and can give us a touch of schizophrenia.

The bad news is, when we think lies are the truth, they can dominate our lives and slowly destroy us.

The good news is when lies are exposed, the truth can dominate, dissolve the lies and take us down the path towards finding out who we are. This is what happened that day when I realized "You're an idiot," was a lie and "You're a good teacher" emerged as truth.

Words have the power of life and death.

They can kill us or give us new life.

They can hurt or heal.

It is important to speak life-words to others, especially to the young.

It can have a powerful influence, because it feeds our beliefs.

And belief is a very powerful motivator.

Every step we take is fueled by what we believe.

If we believe a lie, our actions are destructive.

If we believe the truth our actions are productive.

As the truth about the lie became clear, I was getting to the source of who I really was:

I was a good teacher.

I had good skills as a writer and thinker that could be developed.

I was unique and special and did not have to compare myself with others, especially my "genius" siblings.

I had special skills to make a significant contribution to my fellow humans.

Somehow, seeing the "idiot" lie and the "good teacher" truth disarmed the accuser in my brain and I have had peace ever since.

Yes, I have caught myself going back to the old pattern, but the truth has been winning more small battles in the war against deception.

What a relief.

The anger has subsided.

My wife Reenie and I are communicating better.

You want to hear a real marvel?

Soon after I saw the truth, we painted the cement walls in the basement without an argument and with much humor! (Note: cement walls are very porous and suck up paint like a sponge. You have to slap it on, and in the process, we were covered with white paint.) Knowing how hard it was for us to work together in the past, I rate that as a miracle! You see, I no longer imagined her requests were followed by the tag line "you idiot" – as in "hand me the paint – you idiot."

If you are in a similar place with anger, fear, discontent, insecurity, loneliness, irritability, or thoughts of suicide, listen to the words you are saying to yourself.

Become the observer of your thoughts.

Let your True Self separate the lies and truth.

Trust your instincts on this.

Then believe the truth.

Welcome to freedom!

As I have shared this breakthrough with others, the response has been astounding. Many have shared their deep fears and doubts. It seems most of us carry around unconscious lies that have profoundly affected our lives.

One very sweet lady wrote that she has dealt with rage for years and is excited to get to the root. Knowing her, I was surprised to hear she used the word "rage." She seemed to come across as a gentle person.

Another man became aware that he was calling himself an idiot when he made a mistake fixing something.

One man heard, "Why can't you be like your brother?" and has spent his life comparing himself with others.

The amazing thing is that this all came from people who knew in their minds that these things weren't true. If you asked the man who made a mistake if he was stupid, he would say, "Of course not. I got my doctorate from Indiana University." And he would be right, because I know he is a very smart man, widely read, and a good thinker.

If you asked me if I believed I was an idiot, I would say, "No, of course not. I graduated from the University of Kansas in Political Science and Philosophy, and have written several books."

So what is going on here?

Why did I think I was an idiot for sixty-eight years as a college graduate?

Because destructive emotions were feeding my thoughts, and were drowning out the truth in my heart.

We must "see" with the heart, not just reason in our mind.

Our heart is the source of who we really are.

Irrational emotions and can subconsciously overpower our rational minds.

This cosmic battle between lies and truth is fought in:

Every person,

Every group,

Every culture,

Every nation,

Every religion,
Every government,
Every family.

We all know the agony of people hearing things we are not saying. And we hear things others are not saying. Like when I hear my wife say, "Turn right, you idiot!" when she was just saying "turn right." This is going on all day in all our lives, because our Imposter is whispering (or shouting) his lies from our past through our emotions. It is the cause of most of the anger and division in the world.

Think of cultures that have been at war for centuries that can't even remember how the division started. The hate continues anyway.

What if we all began speaking the truth from our real self that is in line with the rhythms of the universe? Then truth will change the world and set it free from the darkness of lies.

"Truth is within ourselves; it takes no rise
From outward things, whatever you may believe.
There is an inmost center in us all,
Where truth abides in fullness; and around,
Wall upon wall, the gross flesh hems it in,
This perfect, clear perception – which is truth.
A baffling and perverting carnal mesh
Binds it, makes all error; and to KNOW
Rather consists in opening out a way
Whence the imprisoned splendor may escape,
Than in effecting entry for a light
Supposed to be without."

(From Paracelsus by Robert Browning)

Vibes

"Men saw this mask, but the bishop saw his face. Men saw his life, but the bishop saw his conscience."

(Victor Hugo, "Les Miserables")

So get this scene.

Someone is heaping flattery and praise on you, but you sense something is not right. You are waiting for the other shoe to drop. You are wondering what they want from you. Like an old mentor of mine said, "Beware when someone slaps you on the back; he may be trying to get you to cough up something."

Or how about this?

Someone is making suggestions about your prized painting, but you are not upset with the criticism, because you sense sincere love and respect behind their words.

Or this...

You are listening to a charismatic speaker pitch a "can't lose" investment opportunity. The testimonies are convincing. The audience is enthusiastic. You are hearing all the right words, but you sense something is wrong. You can't put your finger on it. You can't define it. Despite enormous peer pressure, you decided not to invest. Months later you hear it was all a slick fraud and many have lost millions. Your inner voice saved you from a huge loss.

Or more critically...

A mother senses tragedy the moment her daughter has an accident miles from home.

What is happening here?

Vibes!

Quantum Physics has taught us that what we see is not really what is. What we see as solid matter is made up of tiny particles of electromagnetic energy. What looks solid is actually made up of energy fields.

We are all putting out vibes of energy that speak much louder than our words. We project love, hate, depression, joy, peace, agitation and fear, to those around us.

The vibes with which we communicate are more important than the words we say.

The same words can be spoken in a spirit of love or hate, sadness or joy, lies or truth. It is estimated that 93% of all communication is nonverbal.

In the cases above, vibes were more powerful than words.

My mom never called me an idiot. In fact, she tried to convince me I was as smart as my brother and sisters. But her vibes spoke something else. I knew I was not measuring up to her expectations. I sensed she was embarrassed talking to her friends about my lack of success in school. Her words could not overcome her vibes that I was "below standard." She told me I had a great smile and personality trying to make me feel good, but I sensed she thought I had below average scholastic ability. Several times she suggested careers that did not require much intelligence.

Children do not understand Quantum Physics, but know all about vibes. They sense when our words do not match our hearts. They know intuitively when we are not what we say we are.

The adult word for this is hypocrisy.

Someone has said there are two groups you cannot fool: prisoners and children.

They sense vibes.

When I was on the road for Rachel's Challenge, speaking to children and teens, I knew I could not hide my vibes. If I did not love and respect them, my words would fall to the ground before reaching their ears.

They knew if I was a fake.

I knew I had to be myself, not an actor trying to impress them. It was an accountability factor for me. I knew my vibes were speaking louder than my words. I knew my vibes were speaking in all my relationships, not just kids. I had to be transparent in order to communicate authentically.

To read vibes correctly, we must have enough detachment to step back and discern any hidden agendas or ulterior motives. It takes time, and often failure, to develop discernment.

Advice from trusted friends who have experienced hurt themselves can help us.

Past pain can make us more sensitive to possible future hurt.

A few years ago, I was hurt when a "control freak" took over a group I was leading and forced me out. I was angry at myself for letting him do it to me without a fight. I spent many months apologizing to people in the group for letting it happen.

Later, another "control freak" came along and I recognized his destructive motives before he said two sentences. The previous experience made me sharper to discern the next attempt and I did not let it happen again. My instincts had been honed by painful experience. My "vibe-detector" was fine-tuned from past pain.

Jacques Lysseyran, "blind hero of the French resistance" during World War II, discovered the power of vibes when he became blind as a boy. He was born in Paris in 1924 and when he was eight, he fell against the corner of a school desk, damaged his optic nerve and became totally blind. He was fifteen at the time of the German occupation. Because he was blind the Volunteers' Central Committee insisted he be in charge of the delicate and dangerous job of recruiting for the resistance movement. He had "the sense of human beings" and "could hear more accurately and pay better attention". He saw men through the tones of their voices, through some sense that sighted people lacked. He was nearly infallible in judging people. I say "nearly" because one time he went against his instincts and admitted a man of whom he was not absolutely sure. This man later betrayed him and he was sent to a concentration camp.

He writes, *"They told me that to be blind meant not to see. Yet how was I to believe them when I saw. After my operation I tried to use my eyes, and after much anguish, I realized I was looking in the wrong direction... I was looking too far off, and too much on the surface of things. At this point some instinct made me change course. I began to look more closely, not at things but at a world closer to myself, looking from an inner place to one further within, instead of clinging to the movement of the world outside. The substance of the universe drew together, redefined and peopled itself anew... My blindness had thrown my head against the humming heart of things, and the heart never stopped beating... The waves were arranged in steps, and together they made "one music."*

Did you hear that?

He "saw" vibes looking from an "inner place."

This inner place is the source of our true person.

It sees through the outer illusions to the inner reality of others.

But there was something that could block the light in his heart...

He explains that anger and frustration could shut off his sensitivity to reality. *"Anger and impatience threw everything into confusion. The minute before I knew where everything was in the room, but if I got angry, things got angrier than I. When I was playing with my friends, if I suddenly grew anxious to win, to be first at all costs, then all at once I could see nothing... I could no longer afford to be jealous or unfriendly, because a bandage came down over my eyes, and I was bound hand and foot and cast aside."*

Does it sound "far out" that things in the room could get angry at him?

Not if you understand that the entire universe is vibes.

Jacque learned that our vibes can change how the universe responds to us.

Speaking about Jacques' anxiety to win blinding his instincts... Athletes can tell you that thinking about winning can cause them to lose. When the Denver Broncos returned from a sound beating from the Dallas Cowboys in the Super Bowl, placekicker, Jim Turner said, "We were thinking about winning. They were thinking about football."

I can identify. When I was taking tests in school, I was thinking about passing (winning) and less on the questions I needed to answer. Trying to pass (win) undoubtedly knocked down my scores which reinforced the lie that I was stupid.

So what's the point?

Our Imposter is sending out vibes giving a false impression of who we are. The problem is compounded when we are in contact with the vibes of other Imposters around us. Inaccurate readings are floating in the air like smog. This is why a party can seem so fake and superficial. False judgments are hindering relationships. The entire scene is a distasteful illusion, and we feel stuffed in a bag with no air. Our impulse is to run outside and get some fresh air.

Smog banks of impostor vibes are clouding meetings, conversations and relationships all over the world. Governments are blinded and choked by them from the halls of Congress to meetings at the Kremlin. Families and spouses can't understand each other. I think it can be safely said that clashes between Imposters is the root cause of most conflict. When an Imposter responds in kind to another, it escalates the conflict.

Why is this? Because, among other things, Imposters have to:

Appear good on the outside – conforming to the group to be accepted.

Protect themselves from pain – by flight into isolation or by fighting back.

Be right and know it all – never admitting wrong and blaming others.

Stay in control – by resisting surrender and bullying others.

Promoting hidden agendas – by working the system for personal advantage.

Remain undisturbed in their opinions, doctrines, and beliefs – by blocking discussion to the contrary.

You want some examples of Imposters at work?

OK.

A guy tries to speed around me on a freeway on-ramp in Phoenix. My Imposter has to stay in control, be first and win. So I speed up to cut him off. His Imposter kicks in and he jams it to the floor. We are drag racing to the freeway entrance. He gets in the lead, cuts me off and slams on his brakes – presumably to teach me a lesson not to mess with him. I skid into a fishtail over two lanes of traffic, barely avoiding two collisions. I finally get straightened out and take a deep breath.

I am grateful my Imposter did not kill me and my wife that day!

Stupid?

Yes.

Immature?

Absolutely!

Lesson learned?

Certainly!

What was the lesson?

Take a deep breath and observe what my Imposter is doing before I get nailed.

Here's another example from my Imposter's bag of tricks.

My wife approaches...

"Thought you said you were going to fix that today!"

My Imposter kicks in with irritation.

"No, I said I would work on it when I had time!"

Her Imposter kicks in, having to be right.

"No, you said, 'today.'"

My Imposter, having to be right too, responds with a dodge.

"No, I didn't! You are trying to control me and put a guilt trip on me!"

Knowing my love of truth, her Imposter uses it against me.

"No, I am just telling you the truth. You always say you hate lying!"

I respond with the politics of personal destruction and bullying.

"You're nuts! I never said 'today."

She responds in kind.

"You're stubborn and can never admit when you are wrong."

So you can probably finish the argument from there.

The battle ends with someone, usually me, going silent (which is a weapon, not loving surrender). As someone used to tell me, "There is a big difference between silence and peace!"

Of course, no one wins, because Imposters will not surrender.

This is happening all over the world a million times a day.

As someone has said,

In prisons there are those who live in heaven.

In palaces there are those who live in hell.

Two Conversations

"It is sad to tell; but after having judged society, which has caused the misfortunes, he judged the Providence which created society, and condemned it also. Thus, during those nineteen years of torture and slavery, did this soul rise and fall at the same time. Light entered on the one side, and darkness on the other."

(Victor Hugo, "Les Miserables")

We are all engaged in two conversations:
The outer conversation – what we think is acceptable to say;
And the inner conversation - what we are really thinking.
Outer talk is boring, shallow and lonely.
Inner talk is refreshing, alive and deep.

Sometimes when I stand up to speak, I wonder where the people are. I know they are sitting in front of me, but some seem far away, in another place. They are not "with me" – not on the same train. One time I noticed a man was wearing ear phones while I was teaching. Where was he? The game? Listening to his favorite song? Talk radio? I knew where he wasn't – he wasn't with me! Most people are not that blatant but can be just as far away in their minds. Maybe that guy was more honest than the rest, because he let me know what he really thought of my talk.

We all are a little like that man - listening to our inner ipods while talking to others.

We are not "there" with them, but someplace else – thinking of the past, what to do next, or just thinking the whole scene is boring.

Sometimes when I am talking to a person with that faraway look, I stop and ask, "Where are you."

Why keep talking if no one is listening?

We need to have and be a "listening ear" to have true communication.

Good listeners are very rare, but extremely valuable.

I meet with a small group of men who have taken the risks of inner conversation. It is the most valuable fellowship I have. We are on a journey to deeper honesty. We are not there yet, but on our way. There is something healing about realizing we are all struggling with similar things.

"So what is it that helps people? Certainly not advice, for they either accept it blindly, or reject it. In either case it does no good. What helps people is what helped me, that is to say an encounter with people who talk honestly about their own distress, their difficulties, their frustrations, their rejections, and their evasions." (Psychologist Dr. Paul Tournier)

Not only do we need other's listening ears, we need to listen to ourselves to discern the truth from the lies. The problem is we modern people lack silence. We no longer lead our own lives, but are dragged along by events. We do not quiet ourselves enough to give our True Self a chance to speak. The voice of our Imposter is yelling so loud, we can't hear ourselves think. The Observer in us is speaking, but we can't hear. This is why our thoughts and story hijack our identity and we don't know who we are. In all the noise, we become alienated from ourselves.

However, it is obvious that we crave conversations on and honest level.

I believe the appeal of great writers like Tolstoy, Dickens,

Dostoevsky, Melville, Hugo, etc. is that they tell of the inner conversations people are having. We are able to identify with the "sub texts" in the mind of the characters.

I love the thoughts of the prince in "War and Peace," when he is forced to attend a party against his wishes. He is having inner conversations that are socially unacceptable, and so must remain muted. His thoughts are so like mine when I do not want to be at a social event. Sometimes someone bursts out with what he is really thinking and is thought to be crazy. The outer conversation has become the convention.

Of course, I am not saying we are to blurt out all our inner conversations. That would be foolish and even destructive. What I am saying is we need to recognize there are two conversations going on in us and to discern which parts reflect who we are and which don't. If we adopt social conventions as our identity, then we are letting our Imposter dominate us.

Sometimes truthful inner conversations are blurted out in public especially, from children.

I read of a solemn church service in France. The priest was walking slowly back and forth in his vestments and chanting the Eucharist. All of a sudden a little five year-old girl asks her father in a loud voice, *"Daddy, what are those people doing up there?"* The inner conversation blasted through the outer shell and touched everyone with a little glimpse of reality.

Of course, the child did not know what she was doing. She was just being herself, as children do. This is where we all start – as children being real, but slowly the culture "trains" us to "act right." As we grow into adults, we all become performers on a stage playing an acceptable part. We lose the transparency of our childhood. The child's outburst becomes just a distraction from the ceremony of lifeless form.

Why do we love the children's concerts? It certainly is not

because of the quality of the music. It's off key, out of rhythm, and half the kids are doing something else. But the parents love it and crowd around the stage taking pictures like a bunch of paparazzi chasing a rock star.

I think we love kids, because they are themselves. They are "real" like we want to be, but can't, because it is socially unacceptable. Children take us back to the freedom of "the way we were."

On a beautiful winter day, I decided to walk to the grocery store. It's about three miles round trip and perfect exercise. Part of my route took me along the way I used to walk our 7 year-old granddaughter, Amelia, to school. Those times were special watching her skip along, joyful, excited and spontaneous – jumping into snow piles. She was not concerned about government corruption, economic down times, or possible tornados in the Midwest, like I was. She had quickly forgotten past disappointments. She was living in the moment, not worried about the future except to dream of going to Museum of Nature and Science to see the dinosaurs. She loves dinosaurs!

Children live like we are supposed to live – childlike. They are resilient and live from moment to moment.

We all start out that way – unique, spontaneous, and special. I know I did. My greatest joy was riding my "four wheeler" up and down the terraces at our home in Kansas City. I was unaware of the problems my parents had living with my grandmother, or mom's struggles taking care of me while dad was in the South Pacific fighting in WWII. I was just "Jimmy."

As with all of us, the world's systems slowly closed in on me and buried my uniqueness and joy. The educational system limited my options and pushed me into categories where I didn't fit. I was labeled "stupid" because I couldn't "keep up," but I just wasn't interested in the program. The political system never gave me something noble to believe in. The religious system only created more and more questions it could not answer.

So I spoke, and even taught others, with borrowed the voices to be accepted.

I was lost, didn't know where I fit, or what my purpose was.

I discovered a new world when I decided to take the risk of transparency. I did not jump in with both feet at first. I had to be wise about what to share. I had to probe a bit and find those who responded with honesty and acceptance. I spent time with those with whom I had favor, and learned to not take it personally if others did not accept me. I have walked this path for many years and have never regretted it despite a few rejections along the way.

The Power of the Collective

"Be it true or false, what is said about men often has as much influence upon their lives, and especially on their destinies, as what they do."

(Victor Hugo, "Les Miserables")

Our Imposter has absorbed many deceptions from a powerful collective mentality that dominates our human existence.

It herds us into groups,
Labels us as categories,
Sees crowds, not individuals,
Stifles distinctive creativity,
Does not respect uniqueness,
And dresses us in uniforms.
Teachers see "students."
Organizers see "workers."
Politicians see "voters."
Businessmen see "consumers."
Pollsters see "opinions."
Brokers see "investors."
Generals see "soldiers."
Doctors see "patients."
Americans see "Russians."
Writers see "readers."

Movie producers see "viewers."

As we wear our uniforms they seem normal, like the familiar clothes we put on every day. We think our uniform is who we are, but they hide our real person. We put on our costume for our part in the play of life. We may be "the man in the grey flannel suit," the revolutionary activist, the computer geek, the politician, the professor and a thousand others, Athletes dress in the uniforms of their school or city and fans buy the tee shirts. We have learned the power of imagery.

The brilliant scientist and philosopher, Blasé Pascal writes, *"Our magistrates have known this mystery of imagery. Their red robes, the ermine in which they wrap themselves like furry cats, the courts in which they administer justice, the fleurs-de-lis, and all such august apparel were necessary; if the physicians had not their cassocks, if the doctors had not their square caps and their robes four times too wide, they would have never duped the world, which cannot resist so original an appearance. If magistrates had true justice, and if physicians had the true art of healing, they would have no occasion for square caps; the majesty of these sciences would of itself be venerable enough. But having only imagery knowledge, they must employ those silly tools that strike the imagination with which they have to deal; and thereby in fact they inspire respect."*

Of course, we all belong to groups and have rolls to play. There is nothing wrong with that. We are legitimately part of groups of students, patients or citizens, but we are a student, a patient and a citizen. In other words, we are unique people within those groups. The trouble comes when we believe the role is our identity. It can be so "us" that when we change roles, we lose our bearings in life. Maybe that was what happened to Junior Seau when he retired from the glamor, money and excitement of pro football. We don't know, but it happens often. Retirement can be traumatic when image has become our identity.

Watching the pretense of men in the 20th century, Malcolm

Muggeridge comments, *"Judges need their wigs and robes, priests their vestments, scholars their gowns - for that matter, hippies their long hair and fancy dress; otherwise the fraudulence of their pretensions would be all too apparent. Similarly the British Raj needed majestic titles, silver thrones, and ceremonial durbars. In my years of journalism, I have never seen authority that did not give off a whiff of decay, or power that was not sawdust stuffed, or glamour without grease-paint. The White House smile! That Kremlin glower!*

Profound insight!

Our education system has left the rails into collectivism. We have gone from teaching the person to focus on the process and now the emphasis is on performance. The system is stifling uniqueness with conformity, curiosity with compliance, and creativity with mechanics. This kind of collective "tracking" in education is counter to the personal-directed methods of the great educators of the past. They recognized the unique interests of each student as the main motivation for learning, and the sure guide for determining purpose.

Do you remember that I was labeled a poor reader and sent to remedial tutoring? Well, let me tell you what happened. Somehow I got a book about mountain climbing called "Annapurna," the thrilling account of Maurice Hertzog reaching the summit of that great peak. Reading that fascinating true adventure turned me into a good reader! The problem was not my reading skills, but being forced to read books I was not interested in. Many students are floundering like me because they are not treated as persons with unique interests. They have been told the lie that they are poor students, when in reality; they are great learners if they get into things that capture their imagination.

Personality tests label us as one of four, six, or eight "types." These can be used to "track" us into careers that do not fit who we are. When I was given one of these tests, they said I would be a good insurance salesman. I tried that for a few months and sold exactly zero policies! And it was actually fortunate, because the company went belly up, and some of my friends would have lost money!

This kind of collective mentality goes against the wisdom of nature.

The other day I was walking by the lake in our neighborhood and saw two ducks with their new baby ducklings. I stopped and watched them. The ducklings were paddling along naturally by instinct. The parents were letting them be who they were – growing into ducks! They were not trying to turn their "kids" into foxes or tigers or beavers! They were letting them "be who they be," while guiding and protecting them. This is the way kids are supposed to grow up, but the collective system is trying to turn them into different creatures and it is not working.

Half of them are dropping out of school, and I don't blame them.

Some drop outs are legendary.

Thomas Edison the great inventor,

Benjamin Franklyn one of America's Founding Fathers,

Bill Gates of Microsoft,

Albert Einstein the greatest scientist of the 20th century,

Walt Disney creator of movies and theme parks,

Charles Dickens legendary author of "A Christmas Carol" and "Tale of Two Cities,"

Ray Kroc of MacDonald's, and Princess Diana.

These men and women could not breathe in a collective system and escaped. They changed the world with their unique gifts. Other dropouts have not been so fortunate ending up as society's outcasts.

It is not fun being turned into something we are not instead of being encouraged to be what we are.

Artists are not fulfilled being insurance salesmen.

In politics, image is reality. The title of Joe McGinnis' book on Richard Nixon's campaign in 1968 says it all, "The Selling of a President." This book makes the point that "In America, the fundamental metaphor for political discourse is the television commercial." In the immortal words of the producer to the floor manager when one of the Nixon commercials was being recorded, "Keep the witch-hazel handy; we can't do the sincerity bit if he is sweating."

The important thing was to keep up the image, no matter what the truth.

Politics has become a science of distorting truth to put leaders in the best possible light or shelter them from an inconvenient or hurtful reality. Our culture has become so used to the "spinning" of truth, we just shrug it off as if to say, "That's just the way it is done."

I no longer listen to politicians who say, "The American people believe… (Fill in the blank); because I am an "American people" and I do not believe what they say I believe! I get angry when my name is being used to support something I don't believe in.

Religion is famous for creating collectives. A notorious "box of belief" becomes the litmus test of the faithful. Leaving the "box of beliefs" means judgment, rejection and even excommunication from the group. We learn how to conform to gain acceptance and end up not knowing who we are.

A leader stands to teach a group, but he gives a message that is not his heart because he has to "speak to the base" to keep his job. He wants to be accepted, so he teaches what he thinks what people want to hear, and compromises his integrity. He did it consistently, hated himself, and eventually burned out and left the group. Why? He succumbed to the power of the collective, and it crushed his spirit. How do I know? He was me!

The power in collective can make us do things we would never do alone.

A fourteen-year-old boy walked out of a loving home and committed a brutal murder with members of a local gang. His parents swear their son would never do such a thing. He never acted like that at home. What happened? In that gang, he came under the power of the collective.

Seventeen men came together under the banner of Marxism. Their movement multiplied into numerous powerful dictatorships that killed over 100 million people in the 20th century. How did so few control so many? They had the power of the collective.

How did "ordinary" citizens become monsters that would facilitate the Nazi death camps? At the Nuremburg war crimes tribunal, the world was astounded to see such "normal" people on trial for the unspeakable crimes of the holocaust. How did it happen? They came under the power of the collective.

A normally responsible teenager drives like a maniac to impress his friends and causes a head-on collision. Five people are killed and three are critically injured. The teen is heartbroken. His life is radically scarred. What happened? He came under the power of the collective.

What is the "collective"? It is a "corpus" and it means "the main body or substance of anything." It is the Latin word from which we get the English word "corporation." It is the body or "person" that individuals become in a marriage, family, group, business, school, gang, political party, country, culture, or a crowd. This new "person" is invisible, but extremely powerful. It is different from any of the members. Each member has to surrender some individuality to fit in with the group. This is normal and healthy to live in community. However, the power of the "collective" can tempt the individuals to surrender their integrity, and this is where it becomes dangerous and destructive. People begin to do things that violate their conscience to fit in with the aims of the "collective."

This power of the "collective" can completely overpower individuals.

Lt. William Calley formed a gang of soldiers in Vietnam. They were convicted of killing innocent civilians in a massacre at My Lai.

Disciplined men, who would not consider such action alone. They came under the power of the "collective."

Political leaders get caught in the power of the "collective." Different speeches have to be crafted for different groups to win their votes. Each "collective" in the voting "base" must be appeased even though the candidate never intends to keep his promises. It's no wonder that our political system is compromised, confusing, and corrupt.

People caught in a "collective" for a long period of time think their actions are "normal." They think they are right and any correction is out of line. In fact, correction is not tolerated and even resisted. A persecution complex can set in and put a group in cement for life. Children grow up in the party of their parents without a second thought, and vote the same all their lives.

It is hard to be real in a collective culture. *"He who aspires to live as a real person and not like an automaton finds himself caught on the rails of a mass society (and standardized religion) against which originality rebels for a time and then grows weary and is extinguished."* (Dr. Paul Tournier)

Many voices have warned us of the collective mentality:

Jacque Ellul, "The Technological Society;"

George Orwell, "1984" and "Animal Farm;"

Aldous Huxley, "Brave New World;"

Ayn Rand, "Atlas Shrugged" and "The fountainhead."

The computer society and communications advances have increased the dangers of the death of individualism.

Ayn Rand writes of the sad end of the individual, *"Destroyed at the whim of some who sat and voted… Who knows by what minds? Who knows whose will had placed them in power? What motive moved them? … Destroyed by the whim of men whom he had never seen and who had never seen those tiers of metal. Destroyed because they so decided. By what right?…*

People said it because other people said it. They did not know why it was being said and heard everywhere. They did not give or ask for reasons... Now, you see, Dr. Sradler, your're speaking as if this book were addressed to a thinking audience. If it were one would have to be concerned with such matters as accuracy, validity, logic and the prestige of science. But it isn't. It's addressed to the public. And you have always been first to believe that the public does not think."

These groupings may be convenient, but the group label never fully defines an individual. It is frustrating for all of us to be categorized, because the labels never quite fit us.

We live in a world of lies, and if we believe them, they can shape our identity and cause us to act in ways that are not "us."

The world around us is constantly sending out vibes that do not match the words.

We are forced into a collective mentality that undermines our individually.

This is how the collective systems of the world lie to us, and if we come to believe those lies (note: "You're an idiot," or "You are a poor reader," or "our tests say you should be in insurance salesman.") we can assume an identity that is not us.

Believing lies can become malignant and lead to destructive behavior and even certified madness. Dr. Samuel Johnson, most famous for his Dictionary of the English Language, used to say if he did not hold on to truth madness would overtake him. Truth was his only path to sanity.

Blasé Pascal, whom I quoted earlier, said truth was his force and if it was lost all was lost.

There has never been a great man who did not love the truth and never a man so despicable as he who gained power and status by lying. Lying is the game of our age, and lies are much more dangerous than the mushroom cloud hanging over our heads.

The irony is that liars, while trying to gain power over others, actually lose power over themselves.

Ayn Rand writes, *"People think that a liar gains a victory over his victim. What I have learned is that a lie is an act of self-abdication, because one surrenders one's reality to the person to whom one lies, making that person one's master, condemning oneself from then on to faking the sort of reality that person's view requires to be faked. And if one gains the immediate purpose of the lie – the price one pays is the destruction of that which the gain was intended to serve. The man who lies to the world, is the world's slave from then on... There are no white lies, there is only the blackness of destruction, and a white lie is the blackest of all... Lies forced you to offer yourself for a public stoning and to throw the stones by your own hand."*

Did you hear that? The liar is enslaving himself while trying to enslave others!

When we lie to be accepted by the system, we give power to the system, and surrender our freedom.

The encouraging thing is eventually the truth always wins over lies. This may sound like a cliché, but it is absolutely true. When lies are exposed and truth is revealed, the battle is won. Our true self hungers for truth and when it is heard in the heart, it drowns out the lies like even a small candle eliminates the darkness.

We can't fight deception with lies, only with truth.

We can't eliminate problems by being anti-problem.

When I concentrate on what not to do, I end up doing it.

I can't say,

"The one thing I won't do today is:

Say I am an idiot,

Eat too much,

Believe I am useless,

Compare myself with others,

Think I am worthless.

Not trying to do something is putting more focus on it, empowers it and assures we will do it.

When I say, "The one thing I will not do today is have a Dairy Queen vanilla cone; I look for Dairy Queens all over town.

Anti-bulling, anti-drug, and anti-abuse campaigns are producing more bullying, drug use, and abuse.

Resisting evil gives it more power.

Evil is overcome by good.

Lies are dissolved by light.

Bullying is overcome by promoting kindness and compassion.

Martin Luther King understood this principle. *"Darkness cannot drive out darkness; only light can do that. Hate cannot drive out hate; only love can do that."*

So as we conclude this chapter, let me suggest a simple exercise that has helped me.

Make a list of what you are thankful for and what you want to see happen in your life.

I start out thankful for things like...

Living in our beautiful state of Colorado in America, a new day, my loyal, beautiful and good wife, a cup of hot coffee with toast and jam, finishing any task big or small, honest friends, writing with cut and paste... and go on from there to many more things I appreciate.

Then I list what I want to see happen: Be a help to the people at Rachel's Challenge, write creative books that help others complete the journey, be a good father and grandpa to the kids, and husband to my wife, lose weight and inches, etc.

Then, when I feel my thoughts sliding into discontent, I get out the list and repeat it – almost daily.

Since I began this practice, my attitude is better. I received thanks for being the help I wanted to be, the kids and I connected in heart this summer, and I have lost 20 lbs., and this book is coming to completion.

Remember to state things in the positive. Not, "I'm glad I don't live in...," or "I wish I wasn't so fat," or "I wish my wife wasn't so..." Thoughts that focus on the negative give them power.

I have discovered that nature has a law of attraction that gives back what we give out – positive for positive, negative for negative.

Anyway, give it a shot and see what happens.

The Four Laws of Being

"He looked into the garden with that absorbed look which studies rather than sees."

(Victor Hugo, "Les Miserables"

We are all human "beings."
We are not human "doings."
We are not human "things."
We are not human "titles."
We are not human "owners."
We are not human "consumers."
We are not just human "workers,"
"clients,"
"students."
"citizens,"
"buyers,"

I could go on and on about how the world defines us, but you get the point.

We must "be" to be authentic and real. This is the only way we can be free and happy. If we play a role that is not us, we are only actors on a stage, and we never know who we are or where we are.

So lets look at the laws of being...

LAW #1: BE WHO YOU BE.

"Jim, don't hide your convictions and beliefs because you fear rejection. If people reject you because of who you are, that is their problem, not yours. We need you to be yourself, so we can grow and be complete." We had been together a long time and I had kept some of my thoughts hidden because I knew my friend would not agree, but he was a little put off with my hiding for fear of rejection. He exhorted me to be who I am, so he could be all he could be. He still doesn't agree with some of my beliefs, but he respects me, and that is freedom.

The interesting thing to me about my friend's exhortation was he felt incomplete when I hid my true thoughts! That is profound.

It's like the instructions when we get on a plane, "put on your oxygen mask first before helping your child." If we don't; we may both die! The oxygen of life is truth. If we are not who we are, we all die. The best way we can help society and those around us is to be who we are, not what the collective tries to make us.

Fear of rejection or even persecution can force us to play a role to fit in and put us in a prison of unreality. I know. I've been there – worrying too much about what people think about me. The following two quotes have been a help to me

The first is from G.K. Chesterton, the great English philosopher and thinker, and the author of many works from mysteries to philosophy. *"How much happier you would be if you only knew that most people cared nothing about you! How much larger your life would be if yourself could become smaller in it; if you could really look at other men with common curiosity and pleasure; if you could see them walking as they are in their sunny selfishness and the virile indifference! You would begin to be interested in them, because they were not interested in you. You would break out of this tiny and tawdry theatre in which your own little plot is always being played, and you would find yourself under a freer sky, in a street full of splendid strangers."*

The second is from Francis Fenelon, a clear thinking philosopher, *"Don't allow yourself to be upset by what people are saying about you. Let the world talk. All you need to be concerned about is doing the right thing. As for what people want, you can't please everybody, and it isn't worth the effort. One quiet moment alone will more than repay you for every bit of slander that will ever be leveled against you. You must learn to love other people without expecting any friendship from them at all. People tend to be quite fickle. They love us and leave us, they go and come. They shift from one position to another like a kite in the wind, or like a feather in the breeze. Let them do as they will. They can do nothing to you without your permission."*

LAW #2: BE WHERE YOU BE

The only time we have is now.

We wander in places where we do not belong – the past and the future. I quote Pascal again, *"We never keep to the present. We recall the past; we anticipate the future as if we found it too slow in coming and were trying to hurry it up, or we recall the past as if to stay it's too rapid flight. We are so unwise that we wander around in times that do not belong to us, and do not think of the only one that does; so vain that we dream of times that are not and blindly flee the only one that is.*

He says we flee the present because it sometimes hurts and we don't want to face it. On the other hand, if we find the present enjoyable we don't want it to slip away and leave the present joy to begin planning how to make it happen again in the future. We project ourselves into a future time we can't control and never are quite sure we will reach.

"Let each of us examine his thoughts; he will find them wholly concerned with the past or the future. We almost never think of the present, and if we do think of it, it is only to see what light it throws on the future. The present is never our end. Thus we never actually live,

but hope to live, and since we are always planning how to be happy, it is inevitable that we should never be so."

That last line is profound.

Since we are always planning to be happy, we are never happy.

Happiness ends up in a future time that is never here.

It's like being excited to get a new book, but never reading it.

I am convinced that the reason we like to engage in dangerous things is because it forces us to totally engage the present tense. When we go bungee jumping, rock climbing, sky diving, or racing cars; we are totally focused on the moment. The adrenalin is pumping, and we have to pay total attention to survive. Some people come to rely on dangerous activities to keep the thrill of the present, but we can experience it right where we are if we pay attention to the beauty and excitement of the present.

Jacque Lusseyran writes about surviving his time in the Buchenwald concentration camp. *"To forget was the law. We had to forget all the missing, the comrades in danger, our families, the living and the dead… Memories were too close to fear. They consume energy. We had to live in the present, each moment had to be absorbed for all that was in it, to satisfy the hunger for life. To bring this about… when a ray of sunshine comes, open out, absorb it to the depths of your being. Never think that an hour earlier you were cold and an hour later you would be cold again. Just enjoy. Latch on to the passing minute. Shut off the workings of memory… Take away from suffering its double drumbeat of resonance, memory and fear. Suffering may persist, but already it is relieved by half. Throw yourself into each moment as if it were the only one that really mattered."*

Notice he talks about how the power of memories can produce fear – like the fear I felt driving into that intersection where I almost got smashed. Some painful memories can add to the suffering. Jacque had to learn to live in the present to survive.

Living in the moment is not just for surviving a concentration camp, but is also necessary for living in a world of painful memories.

LAW #3: BE WHERE YOU FIT.

When I grab a wrench to try to fix something, my wife gets a little nervous, because in the past I have had a tendency to get frustrated, and force things to fit. I have ended up breaking things or striping some threads on a pipe, and making things worse. So my wife says,

"Remember, if you have to force it, it doesn't fit!"

And so it is when we try to jam ourselves in a place where we don't fit.

We end up breaking relationships and stripping others threads – usually because we are frustrated with where we are. We get angry and try to "fix" others to fit our ways – when others do not want us to fix them!

I burned out running a group that looked to me to fix them. In fact, I thought they were paying me to fix them. I found out I couldn't fix anyone – not even myself. So I quit to get free of the burden of fixing people into the mold of our religion.

My next shock was I found out that freedom wasn't easy! The system told me where I had to be and when I had to be there and what I was supposed to do. I did not have to think for myself, just go along with what was expected of me. Now that I was free, I didn't know where to spend my time or what people to meet.

I sought out an old veteran of living free. I knew he had been walking in freedom for a long time. So I asked him, "How do I know where to I spend my time?"

His response has been a light on my trail ever since. He said, *"Go where you find favor."* He explained that he had been close to a group of men for over eighteen years. Then one week his friends were not returning his calls. He became angry and frustrated with his buddies. He finally figured out what was going on. He realized he had given these men all he could and he was being moved on to help others. He realized he was not to take the rejection personally and just go where he found favor. His word of advice has been very valuable in helping me make decisions about where to spend my time. This has helped me go where I fit. When I violate this principle, I get in places that are not me and I am miserable.

I realized that I was to spend time with those with whom I had rapport, and not to worry about the others. Who do I spend time with? There are so many needy people. I have wasted much time trying to force relationships. If it doesn't "click"—move on. As the old saying goes, if one door closes, another is opening. It is very true. Be patient and wait for the open door. It will appear.

When we play a role that isn't us, we are actors in plays with the wrong lines. Malcolm Muggeridge, the English journalist writes in his autobiography, describes this uneasy feeling. *"A scene often comes to my mind, both sleeping and waking – I am standing in the wings of a theater waiting for my cue to go on stage. As I stand there, I can hear the play proceeding, and suddenly it dawns on me that the lines I have learned are not in this play at all, but belong to quite a different one. Panic seizes me; I wonder frenziedly what I should do. Then I get my cue. Stumbling, falling over the unfamiliar scenery, I make my way onto the stage, and there look for guidance from the prompter, whose head I can just see rising out of the floorboards. Alas, he only signals helplessly to me, and I realize, of course, that his script is different from mine. I begin to speak my lines, but they are incomprehensible to the other actors and abhorrent to the audience, who begin to hiss and shout: 'Get off the stage! Let the play go on! You're interrupting!' I'm paralyzed and can think of nothing to do but to go on standing there speaking my lines that don't fit. The only lines I know."* (From "Chronicles of Wasted Time")

Ayn Rand calls actors "second handers." *"They have no self. They live within others. They live second-hand. They live for greatness— in other people's eyes. Fame, admiration, envy — all that which comes from others. Others dictated his convictions, which he did not hold, but he was satisfied that others believed he held them. Others were his motive power and his prime concern.*

They don't ask: 'Is this true?' They ask: 'Is this what others think is true? Second-handers have no sense of reality. He acts, but the source of his actions is scattered in every other living person. It's everywhere and nowhere..." ("The Fountainhead")

If we take the risks of honesty, we will be free to be who we are.

"Being who we be" gets us to who we should be with and where we fit. It is like a filter system that separates us from those who reject and judge us for who we are and unites us with those who accept us for who we are. If we are playing a role that it is not us, we can never find out where we fit. We are actors on a stage living in illusions, not authentic people living in reality.

LAW #4: BE WITH WHO YOU ARE WITH.

Dostoevsky begins his novel, "The Idiot" with these lines. *"If they had both known what was remarkable in one another at that moment, they would have been surprised at the chance which had so strangely brought them opposite one another in the third class carriage of the Warsaw train."*

There are fascinating people all around us - walking in the mall, waiting for the bus, eating in the restaurant, working beside us, in front of us, and living in our family. Everyone has an interesting story to tell, if we take the time to listen.

Do you remember me talking about being at boring social events?

I found a way to turn them into interesting evenings.

First, I had to silence my Imposter and get the attention off myself and impressing others.

Second, I went prepared to listen.

Third, I went armed with questions to get below the surface.

"What is your favorite movie of all time, and why?"

"What is the best book you have read?"

"What are some things that make you happy?"

Years ago I began a tradition at our family birthday parties. I ask the birthday person, "What is the biggest lesson you have learned this past year?" This has initiated some great discussion and cut through any possible boredom.

One New Year's Eve our family gathered in Phoenix at the home of our oldest daughter, Michelle. Earlier in the week we told everyone what we were going to do. Everyone was tell something they appreciated about the other. Alan, our New Zealand son-in-law, prepared by interviewing everyone throughout the week. Others were more spontaneous. We sat in a circle around a chiminea in the back yard on a surprisingly cool evening in Phoenix. Each person received positive feedback from ten others. It was one of the best times our family has ever had together. I still smile at the encouraging things that were said about this old dad and grandpa.

If you are bored with life and want an adventure, get with another person and listen to their story without thinking about what you have to do next. Connect with the person behind the mask. See through to the heart. Listen with sincere care. I guarantee, you will find an infinitely interesting person.

Enjoy the gifts around you.

GIFTS

One afternoon life seemed incredibly tedious.
Man's condition is always the same.
The same cast of characters is always there.
Public pronouncements are empty and shallow.
Thinkers are silenced and hidden from view.
No literature can hold my interest.

Judgments block honesty.
Men travel in herds and follow each other over the cliffs.
Republican herds, democratic herds,
Liberal and conservative herds, orthodox and religious herds
All falling into space pushed by insane credulity.

Reality and uniqueness are in every person,
But we hide from each other from shame and fear.
We can't break through the judgments.

Then I turned in my swivel chair
and looked at the books on the shelf.
I thought of the wonderful ideas
that have enriched my life.
These are my friends:
Blaise Pascal, Malcolm Muggeridge, Leo Tolstoy,
Paul Tournier, Jacque Ellul, Dr. Samuel Johnson, Alexander Solzhentsyn,
Soren Kierkegaard, and hundreds more-
Their discipline to write,
sharing experiences,
and putting them on paper
in the eras of no cut and paste
Are gifts to me.

This person sitting in front of me is a gift.
The time at the park with the kids is a gift.
All people,
All the days,
All the books,
All creation,
All lives,

Are gifts.
Open them carefully.
Save the notes.
Record in your diary
Go slowly.
Enjoy the moment.
Go behind the surface.
And a dark day turns bright.
Mine did!

Lining Up with Nature

"Nature sometimes joins her effects and her appearances to our acts with a sort of gloomy, intelligent appropriateness, as if she would compel us to reflect."

(Victor Hugo, "Les Miserables")

Want to hear something really great?

Our True Self is already one with nature!

We do not have to struggle to be at one with the universe, we are already there.

We are already a part of the "one song." (uni = "one" verse = "song.")

We have what science seeks – the unified theory of the universe.

We can't explain it, but we are there.

We have the unity every heart longs for.

What is so great about being one with nature?

Well, let me tell you…

When we line up with the laws of nature, the entire universe moves to support us in our goals and dreams.

It is called the law of attraction.

Let me give you a small example.

Remember when I instantly became a good reader? I tapped into a desire of my heart. I had stumbled on "Anapurna," and became fascinated with mountain climbing. I read other books about Sir Edmund Hillary climbing Everest for the first time and courageous men climbing K2, the second highest peak in the world. I wanted to climb mountains. I began to dream about it.

Guess what happened?

Within three years I was a climbing guide in Rocky Mountain National Park during my summer breaks from college! It happened with no manipulation of the system, no pleading with important people, and no need to raise money. I was working in Estes Park, Colorado painting cabins. On my days off, I began climbing some the great peaks there – Flattop, Hallett, Otis, Ypsilon, Taylor and Longs Peak, the highest in the Park. I was asked to come back the next summer and be the hiking guide for the YMCA of the Rockies.

And the rest is history.

I led many groups up those majestic peaks, stood at the top, signed the register, enjoyed a sandwich and orange looking down on the beauty around me and wonder how it all happened. I was as happy as I had ever been.

So how did it happen?

The power of the universe lined up behind my desires to make it happen, because my True Self lined up with the ways of nature.

This is a wonderful place to be.

When we tap into our True Self and line up with nature, we sense the oneness of the universe.

Where all of history is moving toward oneness like leaven fills a loaf – hidden but real.

Where the beauty of infinite variety is all around us.

No two blades of grass are alike.

No two trees are alike.

And where no two human beings are alike. Each special and unique with gifts that complement the whole.

The law of reciprocity motivates us to treat others as we want to be treated.

Because we reap what we sow.

We are inspired to cut others some slack because we know we are judged by our own judgments, and measured by how we measure.

This may not sound like a good thing, but this powerful law motivates us to show kindness and compassion to others.

Years ago a man set sail on a passenger ship headed for Europe. He was assigned a roommate who aroused his distrust. So he took his valuables to the steward for safe keeping. He told the steward of his suspicions about his roommate. The steward responded that he understood and would be glad to place his valuables in the ship's safe. Then he added, "Your roommate brought his valuables to me for safe keeping too."

I thought of the words. *"Don't pick on people, jump on their failures, criticize their faults—unless, of course, you want the same treatment. That critical spirit has a way of boomeranging. It's easy to see a smudge on your neighbor's face and be oblivious to the ugly sneer on your own. Do you have the nerve to say, 'Let me wash your face for you,' when your own face is distorted by contempt? It's this whole traveling road-show mentality all over again, playing a holier-than-thou part instead of just living your part. Wipe that ugly sneer off your own face, and you might be fit to offer a washcloth to your neighbor."* (Eugene Peterson)

In nature, the law of compensation is at once a very great comfort and accountability.

It is comforting to me because every person no matter their high or low position is bound by the same law, and binds us together in human experience. Rich kings and every commoner cannot avoid it. *"There is always a leveling experience that puts down the overbearing, the strong, the rich, the fortunate, substantially on the same ground with all others. Nature has written duality into everything: light and dark, heat and cold, ebb and flow of the waves, in male and female... If we empty here, we must fill there. For everything we missed, we gain elsewhere, and where we gain, we lose."* (Emerson)

Every experience comes with polarity - action and reaction.

Emerson writes over a century ago: *"The farmer imagines power and place are fine things. But the President has paid dear for his White House. It has commonly cost him all his peace, and the best of his manly attributes. To preserve for a short time so conspicuous an appearance before the world, he is content to eat dust before the real masters who stand erect behind the throne."*

"This law writes the laws of cities and nations. It is in vain to build or plot or combine against it. Things refuse to be mismanaged long. Though no checks to a new evil appear, the checks exist, and will appear. If the government is cruel, the governor's life is not safe. If you tax too high, the revenue will yield nothing. If you make the criminal code sanguinary (full of bloodshed), *juries will not convict. If the law is too mild, private vengeance comes in."*

In nature <u>everything is connected</u>.

That little flower, while seeming to be isolated, is touching all of nature, by taking its place.

Truth is connected in all history. If I seek truth I am connected to Plato, Aristotle, Jesus, Augustine, Pascal, and Einstein and all those who have sought the truth. I feel a personal connection with writers who have touched my heart with truth. Sometimes, I look up and thank them for their seeking, writing, and discipline which have meant so much to me.

If I write and speak the truth, I am connected with the chain of truth throughout history, and my work will last to help other generations.

The law of connectedness allows me to leave a legacy of significance.

Living out of our True Self we experience the stability of nature in man's confusing and unstable world.

When I look at the mountains here in Colorado, they speak to me of permanence. If I climb Longs' Peak today, I will find the same boulders in the same places as I saw them fifty years ago.

I can trust the steadiness of nature to continue through the abandonment of fickle friends, the lies of power, the deaths of friends, changes in families, and surprises of life.

Living at one with nature, I can count on the rhythms of seasons.

In winter when it appears nothing is happening, but the roots are going down.

In spring when there is a burst of color and blooming flowers and fruits.

In summer when it's time for harvest.

In fall, the time of shedding the old and getting ready for the new.

As the Byrds sang in their hit song of the 60's "Turn, Turn Turn,"

"To Everything (Turn, Turn, Turn)
There is a season (Turn, Turn, Turn)
And a time to every purpose, under Heaven

A time to be born, a time to die
A time to plant, a time to reap
A time to kill, a time to heal
A time to laugh, a time to weep

To Everything (Turn, Turn, Turn)

There is a season (Turn, Turn, Turn)
And a time to every purpose, under Heaven

A time to build up, a time to break down
A time to dance, a time to mourn
A time to cast away stones, a time to gather stones together

To Everything (Turn, Turn, Turn)
There is a season (Turn, Turn, Turn)
And a time to every purpose, under Heaven

A time of love, a time of hate
A time of war, a time of peace
A time you may embrace, a time to refrain from embracing

To Everything (Turn, Turn, Turn)
There is a season (Turn, Turn, Turn)
And a time to every purpose, under Heaven

A time to gain, a time to lose
A time to rend, a time to sew
A time for love, a time for hate
A time for peace, I swear it's not too late."

Contentment is relaxing and enjoying the season we are in.

It is true that nature can be:
Violent and peaceful.
Mild and stormy.
Sunny and cloudy.
Rainy and clear.
Light and dark.

But the wise accept what they cannot change, change what they can, and discern the difference.

We all leave a wake in this life whether positive or negative.

One day I stopped by the lake in our neighborhood and watched one lone duck paddle across the glassy smooth surface leaving a perfect "V" in his wake. It spread out lapping waves on both shorelines. The evening sun amplified the parable I was watching. All of us leave a wake behind our lives – some for good, some for evil and most a combination of both.

Every step we take has consequences that affect others around us. Good and evil acts spread to the shorelines of our influence. Decisions are never totally private affairs. One person can change millions of lives for good or evil. One man, Hitler, started a war that cost the lives of sixty million soldiers and civilians in the wake of his lust for power. One woman, Mother Teresa bound the wounds of one dying man in Calcutta, India and spread love to millions.

We all leave a wake without trying. We don't have to "try" to change the world, we just do. That duck was not thinking about spreading a wake across the lake. He was just looking straight ahead with purpose to reach the other side. Ann Frank, who died in one of Hitler's concentration camps at the age of fifteen, wasn't thinking about changing the world when she wrote in her journals, but "The Diaries of Ann Frank" have touched millions of hearts.

One of those hearts was Rachel Scott the first student killed in the Columbine tradegy. Rachel was influenced by Ann Frank's writings and was inspired to start a chain reaction of kindness that has multiplied to millions of students in many nations around the world. Neither Ann nor Rachel lived long lives. They both died in their teens. But they both left a wake that has influenced millions. It's not how long we live; it's what we do with what we have.

Never underestimate the influence of each step we take.

That duck was reaching his goal one stroke at a time.

Ann and Rachel were writing diaries one word at a time.

Painters paint a picture, one brush stroke at a time.

We don't have to do big things to change the world. The little things we do transform the world with the wake we leave – one stroke at a time – just like that duck.

Of course, we have to face the opposite side of the coin.

The bad news is when we are out of sync with the way things are, we destroy ourselves – usually slowly and painfully, one step at a time. This is what our Imposter does to us – sets us against the way the universe works.

Our outside is at odds with our inside, and divided we fall.

"Every discrepancy between our outward behavior and our inner feelings is both a moral fault and a psychological injury to our personality." (Dr. Paul Tournier)

"The exclusive in fashionable life does not see that he excludes himself from enjoyment, in the attempt to appropriate it. The exclusionist in religion does not see that he shuts the door of heaven on himself, in striving to shut out others. Treat men as pawns and ninepins and you shall suffer as well as they. If you leave out their heart, you shall lose your own... A wise man will extend this lesson to all parts of life." (Emerson)

Seeing Beyond the Imposters

"You have told me that you were the bishop, but that tells me nothing about your moral personality. Now then, I repeat my question – who are you?"

(Victor Hugo, "Les Miserables")

"I believe that there is a great illusion underlying both the despair of the weak and the unease of the strong – and the misfortune of both. This great illusion is the very notion that there are two kinds of human beings, the strong and the weak. The truth is that human beings are much more alike than they think. What is different is the external mask, sparkling or disagreeable, their own reaction, strong or weak. These appearances, however, hide an identical inner personality. The external mask, the outward reaction, deceives everybody, the strong as well as the weak. All men are, in fact, weak. All are weak, because all are afraid. They all are afraid of being trampled underfoot. They are all afraid of their inner weakness being discovered. They all have secret faults; they all have a bad conscience on account of certain acts which they would like to keep covered up. They are all afraid of other men and of God, of themselves, of life and of death. (Dr. Paul Tournier)

So how can we see behind the Imposters around us?

Rachel Scott found the secret at the young age of seventeen. She wrote in her diary about looking beyond appearances. *"It wasn't until recently that I learned that the first and the second and the third impressions can be deceitful of what kind of person someone is. For example, imagine you had just met someone and you spoke with them three times briefly… and they came off as harsh, cruel, stubborn, and ignorant. You reach your judgment based on these three encounters. Let me ask you something… Did you ever ask them what their goal in life was, what kind of past they came from, did they experience love or did they experience hate? Did you look into their soul and not just their appearance? Until you know them, not just their type, you have no right to shun them. Have you looked for their beauty, their good? Have you not seen the light in their eyes? Look hard enough and you will always find a light and you can help it grow if you don't walk away from these first three impressions."*

Rachel cultivated the habit of giving people three chances before drawing any conclusions about their character. She knew that first encounters can be deceptive. If we take the time to look beyond the appearances, we will discover human souls of great value.

One day I decided to watch a football game from a new perspective. Rather than seeing two impersonal forces trying to win a game, I took off their helmets and saw the person. Instead of looking at the uniforms, I saw John, Michael, Jim and Joe – people. It was an amazing shift in my viewpoint. When a player on the opposing team got hurt, I did not gloat, but my heart went out to them and I thought of the painful rehab they were facing.

I entered a new world of seeing people behind the masks.

I had become aware of a new universe sitting right on top of the visible.

I was "seeing through" the visible to the real world.

I was becoming aware of the unity around me.

How do you know when an Imposter is talking to you?
The signs are easy to read –
anger,
frustration,
depression,
blaming others,
hang dog view of life,
feeling worthless,
The "woe is me" of Eeyore,
"The sky is falling" of Chicken Little.
The list is endless
Imposters are easy to detect if we listen to our instincts.

I find it helpful to mentally step back and not respond immediately to an Imposter. For example, my wife, Reenie, discovered one of the deceptions she has absorbed along the way is: "Stupid drivers!" Her Imposter will start saying things like,

"At least you could turn on your blinker and let us know where you are going."

"He sure didn't give us much room."

"I guess the speed limit applies to everyone but him."

Comments like these can make a trip a very negative experience! If I respond in kind saying, "Yeah, that guy is really a stupid driver!" Then things just escalate and we end up mad at every driver on the road. However if I just take a deep breath and wait a minute, her Imposter quiets down, because there is nothing to feed it.

When we are at social gatherings, we can recognize Imposters because they usually speak out of anger, frustration, fear, depression, and other negative emotions. If we can keep from escalating the emotions with gentle questions, interested listening, and loving vibes; it gives the True Self a chance to emerge. It doesn't always happen, but at least we can create an atmosphere where it is possible.

We can make things worse and give more power by responding in kind.

Instead, think of questions to go behind the surface as Rachel Scott did.

Ask them to tell you their story.

Let them express the hurts and pain.

Get to know them.

Be a "see-througher" not a "look-atter."

The Main Battle

When we think of confrontations between family Imposters escalating to the point of break ups and even divorce,

When we think of school shootings growing out of hate from Imposters lies,

When we think of hostilities between nations intensifying through leader's Imposters,

When we think of world leader's Imposters challenging each other with wars in the balance,

It is critically important that Imposters be silenced.

Every act of violence, feeling of depression, desire to take our own lives, crime committed, act of greed, grasp for power, ego inflated arrogance, "we" verses "them," sexual perversion, idol worship, angry confrontation, having to be right no matter the facts, bribe received, judgments by appearance, defining by labels, etc., has a lie behind it feeding our belief system, and what we believe motivates every action we take.

We have to stop smashing signal lights and go to the core.

What do I mean by that?

Let me illustrate.

Bill was driving with Tom to a meeting when suddenly the oil light lit up on the dashboard.

Bill just kept on.

Tom was concerned the engine might freeze up and asked, "Aren't you going to take care of that?"

With a note of impatience Bill said, "Ok, hand me the hammer in the glove box."

Puzzled, Tom fished for the hammer and handed it to the driver wondering what he was going to do.

The driver took the hammer and with a loud crash, smashed the oil light and said, "There, that fixed it!"

He certainly got the light to go off, but, of course, he fixed nothing.

He had to go to the core and fix the leak and add some oil.

All the symptoms listed above are like that oil light. They are only signals of a deeper problem.

I could not fix my anger problem by smashing the signal.

No matter how many times I said to myself,

"I shouldn't get angry."

"Stop that!"

I was just making it worse, because it was the center of attention.

Instead, watch the "signals."

When the anger, depression, disgust, or moodiness starts, view it as a signal not the cause.

Then step back and say, "That's not me."

Be the Observer of your Imposter, and you will have the upper hand.

Then you will bring the light of exposure into the situation and dissolve the darkness

We can't get distracted by the "signals" and miss the main battle.

Here's a story from WWII that applies...

Operation Fortitude was one of the most effective and important deceptions leading to the successful Normandy invasion in World

War II. It was divided into Fortitude North, a threat to invade Norway, and Fortitude South, designed to induce the Germans to believe that the main invasion of France would occur in the Pas de Calais rather than Normandy. The objective was to keep the Germans from increasing their troops at Normandy, and it worked. In fact, the British spy "Intrepid" had so fooled the Germans, they did not accept the invasion was real for two weeks, and they did not send new forces to the area.

Distracting troop forces away from the main battle lines is a classic maxim of war.

I believe mankind has been distracted from the main battle. The cosmic battle is between lies and truth and it affects every act of every person in every age. The victor between lies and truth is the motivator behind every event in world history.

The main battle is not between political systems – Capitalism verses Marxism, Democracy verses Totalitarianism, Big verses Small Government, Liberalism verses Conservatism etc. Systems are only as good or bad as the character of its leaders and citizens.

The main battle is not between religious systems – Christianity verses Islam, Judaism verses Muslim, etc. All religion carries poisons of hypocrisy, conformity for acceptance and a "we" verses "them" mentality. The history of religion is very bloody with plenty of hate.

The main battle is not even between good and evil. Moralism is very selective and can be arbitrary and confusing. What is good to one can be evil to another.

So the main cosmic battle that determines all others is between lies and truth.

It is that simple.

On the other hand if we think of what the world would be like if more and more people operated out of their True Person, already connected in unity, the future would be as bright as a morning sunrise. I have seen it happen in my own home with my wife and with others around me.

I believe that man is coming to the point of saying "no more."
We simply cannot live like this.
Life is not worth living in an Imposters suit.
It is too painful, empty, and depressing.

The good news is we all have been given a "truth detector" in the form of our True Person. He is a trustworthy counselor, if we let him speak. The problem is our sensors have been turned off by the lies of our Impostor.

All over the world, Imposters are confronting Imposters and the truth is being suppressed.

However, we all can take small steps to silence the lies of our Imposter by exposure, and let the Truth emerge.

Every time we
Take the risks of transparency,
Sincerely listen to another's story,
Engage in honest conversation,
See others as gifts, not opponents,
Look past their Imposter to the heart,
Expose a lie in ourselves,
Speak the truth in love,
We claim a little more ground for the truth.
We can win this battle.
We don't have to wait for others to begin the fight.

We can engage and enjoy the changes, right where we are and continue the chain reaction of truth.

That is my sincere hope.

Books Quoted

Ayn Rand. Philosophy: Who Needs It: Signet. 1984. Atlas Shrugged: Signet 1957. The Fountainhead: Signet.

Blasé Pascal. Pencees: Dutton & Co. 1958.

Eckhart Tolle. A New Earth: Awakening to Your Life's Purpose: Penguin Group. 2005.

The Power of Now: A Guide to Spiritual Enlightenment: Namanst. Publishing. 1999.

Francis Fenelon: Let Go. Scroll Publishing 2007

Fyodor Dostoyevsky. The Idiot. Vintage Classics. 2003

G. K. Chesterton. Common Sense 101. Ignatius. 2006

Jacques Lusseyran. And There Was Light: Blind Hero of the French Resistance: An Autobiography. Morning Light Press, 2006

Malcolm Muggeridge. Chronicles of Wasted Time: An Autobiography. Regnery Gateway, 1973

Parker J. Palmer. The Courage to Teach: Exploring the Inner Landscape of a Teacher's Life, 10th Anniversary Edition. John Wiley and Sons. 2007

A Hidden Wholeness: The Journey Toward an Undivided Life. John Wiley and Sons. 2008

Paul Tournier. The Strong and the Weak: Westminster. 1963.

Ralph Waldo Emerson. The Essential Writings of Ralph Waldo Emerson: The Modern Library. 2000.

CPSIA information can be obtained at www.ICGtesting.com
Printed in the USA
LVOW01s0756251013

358397LV00007B/66/P

9 781478 721253